Medical, Genetic & Behavioral Risk Factors of Pomeranians

BY: ROSS D. CLARK, DVM

H. DAVID HAYNES, DVM – LEAD RESEARCH
AND EDITORIAL ASSISTANT
ART J. QUINN, DVM, DACVO – PROFESSOR EMERITUS,
OKLAHOMA STATE UNIVERSITY CENTER
FOR VETERINARY HEALTH SCIENCES
BRAD HOWARD, DVM – RESEARCH ASSISTANT
PAUL SCHMITZ, DVM – TECHNICAL ASSISTANT
JAN COODY, MBA – TECHNICAL ASSISTANT
NITA RITSCHEL – EXECUTIVE ASSISTANT
GERI HIBBLEN JACKSON – PHOTO ACQUISITIONS

LINDA A. CLARK, RVT, AKC JUDGE – PHOTO ACQUISITIONS

Copyright © 2014 by ROSS D. CLARK, DVM. 602439

ISBN: Softcover 978-1-4990-4646-5
EBook 978-1-4931-9842-9

All rights reserved. No part of this book may be reproduced or transmitted in any form or by any means, electronic or mechanical, including photocopying, recording, or by any information storage and retrieval system, without permission in writing from the copyright owner.

Rev. date: 07/11/2014

To order additional copies of this book or other breed books of the 179 AKC recognized breeds by this author, contact: Xlibris LLC
1-888-795-4274
www.Xlibris.com Orders@Xlibris.com

Medical, Genetic & Behavioral Risk Factors of Pomeranians

INSIDE:

I. ORIGIN, HISTORY AND DESCRIPTION

II. RECOGNIZED RISK FACTORS

    CARDIOVASCULAR-
    HEMATOLOGICAL-
    RESPIRATORY
    PREDISPOSITION

    DERMATOLOGICAL ISSUES

    ENDOCRINE-EXOCRINE-
    ENZYMATIC AND/OR HORMONAL
    PROBLEMS

    DENTITION

    MUSCULOSKELETAL AND NEUROLOGICAL

    OPHTHALMIC (EYE PROBLEMS)

    UROGENITAL

    BEHAVIOR TRAITS

III. MISCELLANEOUS FACTS AND RESOURCES

    CANINE HEALTH INFORMATION CENTER HEALTH
    SCREENING FOR POMERANIANS

    NATIONAL BREED CLUB

BY: ROSS D. CLARK, DVM

PREFACE

This book provides you with a through description and positive attributes of this breed including origin, purpose, history, normal heights and weights, acceptable colors and behavioral traits. Our books differ from most books on dog breeds because this book also provides you with a comprehensive and authoritative source of all the known predisposed hereditary health syndromes for the breed. You will find extensive references for each problem described. We also provide the breed club address for this breed and a list of laboratories and organizations that can provide professional help and information.

As a small animal veterinarian, I have always been intrigued by the way dogs have been bred to fill a purpose in life and further impressed that they also tend to love performing that service. Greyhounds and other sight hounds are built for speed with aerodynamic bodies consisting of small head, deep chest, narrow waist and large leg muscles. On the other hand Dachshunds take their name from German words meaning "badger dog" and they use their long nose, long body and short legs to both track, enter and dig into badger dens.

After developing a practice that catered to clients with show dogs, my interest in each breed continued to grow as I studied and observed more and more about the unique predisposition and incidence of health problems in each breed. Breeders of purebred dogs for show were a challenge and inspirational for me to research and help them with their unique health problems. Historically references to hereditary problems are scattered throughout various Veterinary medical texts and journals such as ophthalmology, neurology, gastroenterology, cardiovascular and dermatology. This book, as well as the other books and articles I have written, is researched and compiled with the intention to provide both veterinarians and dog owners with comprehensive and authoritative predisposition information under the breed name.

At the date of this publication, The American Kennel Club Canine Health Foundation and the The Kennel Club of England reports over 400 known hereditary health syndromes throughout the dog kingdom. At the writing of my first book in 1983, less than 50 hereditary issues are able to be predicted and or diagnosed. Sequencing of the canine genome, DNA tests, metabolic testing including blood tests and urine testing; plus, phenotypic examinations such as radiographs, ultrasound, and CERF or OFA eye registry exams by a Board Certified Veterinary Ophthalmologist have advanced the science of breed related health and behavioral problems.

This book will provide veterinarians, researchers, pet owners and breeders with a comprehensive guide to all the known problems veterinarians and dog owners should consider during pet selection and throughout each life stage of our canine friends.

NOTE

The fact that a breed shows many disorders may be more an indication of the extensive research done on that breed than on its comparative soundness of the breed.

Many genetic disorders are common to several breeds. We do not intend to convey severity of incidence by the length of text within a particular breed chapter. One breed may have forty percent incidence and another breed only four percent. If a thorough study has been done to indicate the percentage of incidence, we make note of it; however, please keep in mind the incidence is only an indicator of the dogs tested. A breed for instance may show eighteen percent incidence of hip dysplasia as indicated by OFA, although breeders and veterinarians may not elect to submit radiographs of hips that are so severely dysplastic the owners and their veterinarians knows that there is zero chance to be rated as OFA normal.

Please be aware that we have included and identified anecdotal information, defined by Merriam Webster's dictionary as unscientific observation; however, the observations of breeders and veterinarians with a special interest in the breed will hopefully be converted to scientific research, often underwritten by breed clubs, to confirm or rule out predisposition to breed problems.

You will note that each chapter is thoroughly referenced to help with the reader's research as well as to credit and appreciate the researchers, writers, and breeders that have helped the animal world and mankind by their work with these genetic disorders.

Ross D. Clark, D.V.M.

TABLE OF CONTENTS

POMERANIAN 1
    ORIGIN AND HISTORY 1
    DESCRIPTION 2
    BREEDING AND WHELPING 3
    GROWTH 4

RECOGNIZED RISK FACTORS IN POMERANIANS 4
    CARDIOVASCULAR-HEMATOLOGICAL-RESPIRATORY 4
    DERMATOLOGICAL 5
    ENDOCRINE-EXOCRINE-ENZYMATIC 5
    DENTITION 5
    MUSCULOSKELETAL 5
    NEUROLOGICAL 6
    OPHTHALMIC 6
    UROGENITAL 7
    BEHAVIOR 7
    OLD AGE 7

MISCELLANEOUS FACTS & RESOURCES 8
    CHIC REQUIREMENTS FOR POMERANIANS 8
    NATIONAL BREED CLUB 8

REFERENCES 9
NOTES 11

POMERANIAN

Parti colored Pomeranian

ORIGIN AND HISTORY

The tiny Pomeranian (Pom) of today strongly resembles the larger Arctic dogs and was probably bred down from them. Although their origin is northern Europe, early Greek gems and jars depict a dog much like the Pomeranian of today. Early Pomeranians weighed as much as 30 pounds but it was believed the process of breeding them down in the Baltic region that gave them their name. In 1888 a Pomeranian from Italy was sent as a gift to Queen Victoria of England. The breed became a favorite of the Queen its popularity in England was due to her championing the breed and encouraging the breeding of smaller Poms. In obedience trials, they are often rated top dog, displaying a sheepdog's cunning. Pomeranians come in a wide spectrum of colors. In past years there was controversy about acceptable color.

The Pomeranian is unusually intelligent and one of the hardiest of the Toy breeds. They are quite vociferous, making alert little watch dogs and companions.

Black and tan and white Pomeranians

DESCRIPTION

The revised (1991) Standard accepts any solid color or any solid color with lighter or darker shadings of the same color, any solid color with sable or black shadings, parti-color, sable and black and tan. The average weight is between 3 to 7 pounds with the ideal show weight being between 4 to 6 pounds. An average height at the withers of 6 inches has been suggested but is not part of the standard.

Some of the more serious faults in the breed are domed skull, too large and low set ears, undershot mouth, light eye rims, light or Dudley nose, out at elbows, down in pasterns, cow hocks, loose patellas, soft open coats and solid-color dogs with white chests or white front legs. Dewclaws on rear legs should be removed at 4 to 5 days. Removal of front dewclaws is optional.

Red sable Pomeranian in show coat

BREEDING AND WHELPING

Pomeranian bitches follow the usual pattern of estrus and gestation, but they require more time to whelp than some breeds. Live whelps may be delivered after many hours of light to moderate contractions. Too many bitches are rushed into delivery with shots or cesarean sections. An average litter of Pomeranians consists of three puppies, each weighing from 3 to 5 ounces. Their color at birth ranges from a mixture of black, brown and gray to clear colors such as orange, black or white.

Some puppies may be as tiny as one ounce at birth and should be watched carefully the first few days. Sometimes they are unable to nurse because the nipples of the dam are too large for their mouths. Even though Poms are an unusually hardy breed for their size, newborns need much attention the first 2 to 4 weeks. Some breeders report the occurrence of puppies seemingly uninterested in eating. These should be checked to see if the tongue is clamped to the roof of the mouth. As they appear unable to relax enough even to nurse, hand feeding is necessary with these puppies. Some bitches will not have enough milk and the puppies should be supplemented with hand feedings.

Black and tan and sable Pomeranian puppies

GROWTH

Puppies vary greatly in their rate of development. The average Pom weighs about 5 pounds at maturity; the skeletal growth is usually complete by 7 months. The weight limit for show adults is from 3 to 7 pounds, with 4 to 5 pounds considered ideal.

RECOGNIZED RISK FACTORS IN POMERANIANS

CARDIOVASCULAR-HEMATOLOGICAL-RESPIRATORY

Patent ductus arteriosus (PDA) with a left to right shunt is the most common cardiac anomaly seen in the Pomeranian. [10,11,12,13,14,15,16] **Tetralogy of Fallot** [27] has also been reported in the breed.

As with other toy breeds, older male Pomeranians have a higher incidence of **myxomatous atrioventricular valvular degeneration.** [26, 27] Mucopolysaccharide infiltration of the valve leaflets causes them to thicken and stiffen. This causes regurgitation of blood into the atrium resulting in a systolic murmur and congestive heart failure in severe cases.

Sick sinus syndrome has been reported in older Pomeranians. This is a disease of the SA node resulting in varying dysrhythmias including sinus bradycardia, alternating bradycardia-tachycardia, sinus arrest, atrial flutter, sinoatrial block, transient asystole and idioventricular rhythm. Symptoms include lethargy, weakness, syncope and Stokes-Adams seizures. Sudden death is uncommon. Antiarrhythmic drugs may be used initially but permanent artificial pacemakers are usually necessary for long-term management. [35]

Methemoglobinemia due to a deficiency of Methemoglobin reductase is a rare hematological condition that has been recognized in Pomeranians. [26] Treatment is unnecessary and affected dogs have a normal life expectancy.

Cyclic hematopoiesis [33(461)] has been reported in Pomeranians. This condition inhibits the neutrophil's ability to kill bacteria. Affected puppies may exhibit signs of fever, diarrhea, joint pain and anemia as early as 8-12 weeks of age.

Tracheal collapse [5,6,7,8] is a condition commonly seen in Pomeranians. The condition is exacerbated by obesity so weight control must be a part of any management protocol.

DERMATOLOGICAL

Pomeranians are subject to three hormone-related dermatopathies each of which present with similar symptoms. **Hyposomatotropism**[26, 28] (pseudo-Cushing's syndrome), **hypogonadism** and **adrenal sex hormone imbalance** all produce coat changes that begin with the loss of primary hair coat while the secondary coat remains, giving the dog a puppy-like appearance. This is followed by symmetrical alopecia and pigment change.

These conditions occur predominantly in male dogs. Hyposomatropism may be caused by low or fluctuating levels of growth hormone while abnormal levels of sex hormones are implicated in Hypogonadism and Adrenal Sex Hormone Imbalance. Elaborate endocrine panels may aid in diagnosis. Castration is the initial treatment of choice for Hypogonadism and Adrenal Sex Hormone Imbalance in intact male dogs. If this is not possible or there is no response, supplementation with appropriate hormones including growth hormone is indicated. Melatonin has been suggested as a treatment for Adrenal Sex Hormone Imbalance as it is known to suppress endogenous progestins. These conditions are referred to by breeders as "elephant skin or black skin.[9]

Sebaceous adenitis[31b] has been identified in the breed. This is a keratinization disorder characterized by the destruction of sebaceous glands. Affected dogs have areas of alopecia and inflammation with greasy skin and tightly adhering scale.

ENDOCRINE-EXOCRINE-ENZYMATIC

Pomeranians appear to have a higher risk of **hyperandrogenism.**[26] High levels of testosterone and its derivatives and produce multiple symptoms including aggression, virilization of female dogs, enlargement of genitalia and the prostate, alopecia hyperpigmentation and Tail gland hyperplasia.

Hypothyroidism occurs in the breed.[26] 2.5% of the Thyroid panels submitted to the OFA were abnormal.[30]

DENTITION

Oligodontia (missing teeth) and **prognathism** (under shot jaw) are seen in Pomeranians.[33]

MUSCULOSKELETAL

According to statistics kept by the Orthopedic Foundation for Animals (OFA), Pomeranians are ranked first in the number of examined dogs affected with **patellar luxation** (41.1% abnormal).[1, 2, 3, 4, 30]

Based on a breed susceptibility study, the Pomeranian is at increased risk for **ununited anconeal process.**[37]

Legg-Calve'-Perthes disease has been reported in Pomeranians. This is the aseptic necrosis of the femoral head and neck. The disease is usually unilateral with onset between 4 and 12 months of age. A recessive mode of inheritance with incomplete penetrance is suspected. The OFA ranks the breed 3rd with 2.9% of the evaluations being abnormal.[30, 33]

Shoulder dislocation has been noted in the breed.[17, 18] The shoulder usually luxates medially (toward the body).

NEUROLOGICAL

Ununited fontanels (Patent molera) are found in Pomeranians increasing their risk of cerebral trauma. While **hydrocephalus** [26] does occur in the breed, open fontanels are not necessarily an indication of that condition.

Globoid cell leukodystrophy is a lysosomal storage disease that occurs in Pomeranians. [29]. A defect in the enzyme Beta-galactosidase allows for the accumulation of Galactocerebroside in macrophages of the white matter resulting in ataxia, tremors, progressive paraparesis and impaired vision. It is seen in Pomeranians at about 1.5 years of age.

Pomeranians are predisposed to **atlanto-axial subluxation** [19, 20, 21, 22, 23] due to a **congenital absence of the dens.** [31] This results in compression of the cervical spinal cord with symptoms ranging from neck pain to quadriplegia.

Intervertebral disk disease occurs in the Pomeranian. [33(95)]

OPHTHALMIC

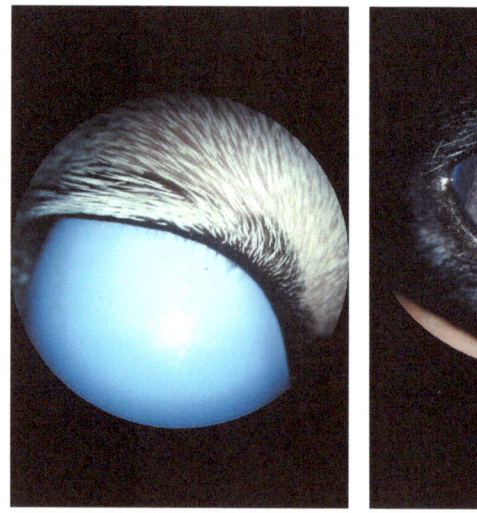
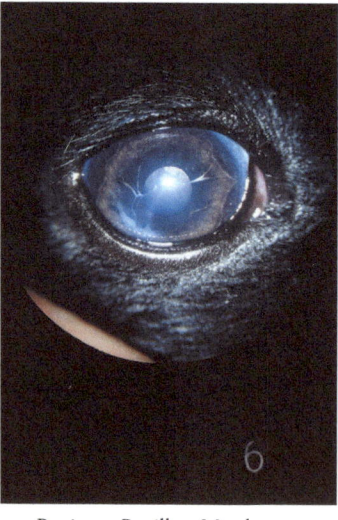
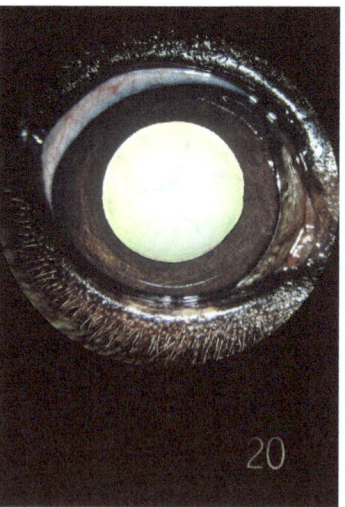

Distichiasis; Note the presence of eyelashes directed toward the cornea

Persistent Pupillary Membranes

Cataract

Distichiasis refers to eyelashes abnormally located on the eyelid margin in the Pomeranian. This may occur at any age and can cause corneal irritation. [32]

The Pomeranian is at increased risk for medial canthal **entropion.** [32, 33(903)] Entropion is a conformational defect resulting in the in-rolling of one or both of the eyelids which may cause ocular irritation. It is believed to be inherited as a polygenic trait.

Persistent pupillary membranes (PPM) are vascular remnants found in the anterior chamber and fail to regress after birth. Depending on location and size, they may cause vision impairment. Iris to iris PPM occurs in the Papillon. [32]

Cataracts have been added to the list of ocular disorders seen in the Pomeranian. [32] A cataract is defined as a partial or complete opacity of the lens or its capsule, which if complete can cause blindness.

Vitreous degeneration has also been recently reported in Pomeranians.[32] Vitreous degeneration is the liquefaction of the vitreous gel that can predispose the eye to retinal detachment or glaucoma.

Progressive retinal atrophy (PRA) refers to the degeneration of the photoreceptor cells (rods and cones) leading to blindness. PRA with an onset of 5-6 years has been reported in this breed.[33(906)]

UROGENITAL

Pomeranians have an increased incidence of **dystocia** due in part to the head shape of the puppies.[25] **Cryptorchidism**[26] is seen in Pomeranians.

BEHAVIOR

The Pomeranian is an excellent companion dog. He is lively, intelligent and affectionate. He is very clever and can be taught tricks very easily. Surveys of veterinarians in Japan and the USA rank the Pom as high in reactivity (excitability, barking, snapping at children and demand for affection). Watchdog traits (barking and territorial defense) are well above average but owner dominance is only average. They are considered to be of low to medium trainability. Pomeranians are not a good choice for families with small children as they are rated in the highest percentile in the snapping at children category. [38, 39]

OLD AGE

A Pomeranian may live as long as 15 or 16 years. The senior dog slows down just as an older human being does. They are subject to heart and kidney trouble, cataracts and deafness. The dogs suffer from prostate problems, and the bitches from metritis. Their diets should be softer to compensate for loss of teeth. Teeth are lost mostly from plaque build-up. Regular dental care will help prevent this. A survey of the Veterinary Medical Database indicated that gastrointestinal disorders and trauma were the most commonly diagnosed causes of death in teaching hospitals.[36] A survey of Pomeranian owners conducted via the OFA indicated that respiratory, orthopedic and dermatological disorders were the most frequently diagnosed health problems in the breed.[30]

MISCELLANEOUS FACTS & RESOURCES

Health screening tests recommended for Pomeranians by the Canine Health Information Center (CHIC)

Here is how CHIC works to help dog fanciers to improve their breeds

CHIC works with national breed clubs, the AKC Canine Health Foundation and the Orthopedic Foundation for Animals (OFA) to create a list of health screening procedures designed to eliminate inherited health problems from dogs used for breeding. The procedures vary from breed to breed and may change if new problems are identified or new tests become available. A dog must have completed all the required health screening procedures in order to receive a CHIC number. For more information contact: www.caninehealthinfo.org/

CHIC REQUIREMENTS FOR POMERANIANS

Eye Exam by a boarded ACVO Ophthalmologist: Results registered with CERF or OFA
Congenital cardiac Database: OFA evaluation a follow up evaluation is recommended between 3 and 5 years of age
Patellar Luxation: OFA evaluation
Hip Dysplasia (Optional): OFA evaluation
Legg-Calve' Perthes (Optional): OFA evaluation
Autoimmune Thyroiditis (Optional): OFA evaluation from an approved laboratory Recommended testing at 1, 3 and 6 years of age [34]

NATIONAL BREED CLUB

The National Breed Club is a good place to discover all the things you can do with your Pomeranian and to contact other Pomeranian owners.

AMERICAN POMERANIAN CLUB, INC
www.AmericanPomeranianClub.org

References

1. Knight, G.C. "Abnormalities and Defects in Pedigree Dogs III: Tibio-femoral Joint Deformity and Patella Luxation," *J. Sm. Anim. Prac.*; 1963: 4:463-464.
2. Kodituwakku, G.E. "Luxation of the Patella in the Dog," *Vet. Rec.*; 1962: 74:1499-1507.
3. Loeffler, K. and Meyer, H. "Hereditary Luxation of the Patella in Toy Spaniels," *Vet. Bull.*; 1962: 32:1703; 1962
4. Priester, W.A. "Sex, Size and Breed as Risk Factors in Canine Patellar Luxation," *JAVMA*; 1972: 160:740-742.
5. Done, S.H., Clayton-Jones, D.G., Price, E.K. et al "Tracheal Collapse in the Dog: A Review of the Literature and Report of Two New Cases," *J. Sm. Anim. Prac.*; 1970: 11:743-750.
6. Leonard, H.C. "Collapse of the Larynx and Adjacent Structures in the Dog, "JAVMA; 1960: 137:360-364.
7. Leinard, H.G. "Surgical Correction of Collapsed Trachea in Dogs," *JAVMA*; 1971158:598-600.
8. O'Brien, J.A., Buchanan, J.A., Kelly, M.A. "Tracheal Collapse in the Dog," *J. Am. Vet. Rad. Soc.*; 1966: 7:12-l 9.
9. *American Kennel Club Gazette*. Pomeranian column. Dec. 1990: 132.
10. Patterson, D.F., Pyle, R.L., Buchanan, J.W. "Hereditary Cardiovascular Malformation of the Dog: Birth Defect," Original article series in XV Cardiovascular System. National Foundation, 1973: 100-l 74.
11. Kirk, R.W. and Bistner, S.I. *Handbook of Veterinary Procedures and Emergency Treatment: Hereditary Defects of Dogs*. 1975: Table 124, 661.
12. Mulvihill, J.J. and Priester, W.A. "Congenital Heart Disease in Dogs: Epidemiologic Similarities to Man," *Teratology*; 1973: 7:73-78.
13. Patterson, D.F. "Epidemiologic and Genetic Studies of Congenital Heart Disease in the Dog," *Circ. Res.*; 1971: 23:171-202.
14. Patterson, D.F. 'Canine Congenital Heart Disease: Epidemiological Hypotheses," *J. Sm. Anim. Prac.;* 1971: 12:263-2287.
15. Mulvihill, J.J. and Priester, W.A. "The Frequency of Congenital Heart Defects (CHD) in Dogs," *Teratology*; 1971: 4:236-237.
16. Patterson, D.F., Buchanan, J.W., Trautvetter, E. Abt, D.A. "Hereditary Patent Ductus Arteriosus and its Sequelae in the Dog," *Circ Res.;* 1971: 29:1-l 3.
17. Campbell, J.R. "Shoulder Lameness in the Dog," *J. Sm. Anim. Prac.*; 1968: 9:189-l 98.
18. Vaughn, L.C. and Jones, G.D.C. "Congenital Dislocation of the Shoulder Joint of the Dog," *J. Sm. Anim. Prac.*; 1969: lO: l-3.
19. Downey, R.S. "An Unusual Cause of Tetraplegia in a Dog," *Canad. Vet. J.* 1967: 8:216-217.
20. Geary, J.C., Oliver, J.E., Hoerlein, B.F. "Atlanto-axial Subluxation in the Canine, "*J. Sm. Anim. Prac.*; 1967: 8:577-582.
21. Ladds, P., Guffy, B., Blauch, B. *et al:* "Congenital Odontoid Process Separation in Two Dogs," *J. Sm. Anim. Prac.*; 1970: 12:463-471.
22. Parker, A.J. and Park, R.D. "Atlanto-axial Subluxation in Small Breeds of Dogs: Diagnosis and Pathogenesis," *VM/SAC*; 1973: 68:1133-l 137.
23. Erickson, F., Saperstein, G., Leipold, H.W. "Congenital Defects in Dogs: A Special Reference for Practitioners," Ralston Purina Co.; (reprint from *Can. Prac*, Veterinary Practice Publishing Co.; l978)
24. Magrane, W.G. *Canine Ophthalmology*, 3rd ed. (Lea & Febiger, Philadelphia, PA., 1977); 305.
25. Hahn, S. "Variation of Skull Traits and Reproduction in Breeds of Small Dogs," Thesis, Tierarztliche Hochschule Hannover, Ger. Fed. Rep. 1988: 130; 111 ref.
26. Tilley, Lawrence P., Smith, Francis W.K.Jr, The 5 Minute Veterinary Consult; Canine and Feline, 4th ed. Ames, IA, Blackwell Publishing 2007
27. Kittleson, Mark D., Kienle, Richard D. Small Animal Cardiovascular Medicine. St. Louis, MO, Mosby Inc. 1998

28. Scott, Danny W., Miller, William H. Jr., Griffin, Craig E. Muller and Kirk's Small animal dermatology-5th ed. Philadelphia, PA: W.B. Saunders Co. 1995
29. Oliver, John E. Jr., Lorenz, Michael d., Korngay, Joe N. Handbook of veterinary neurology, 3rd ed. Philadelphia, PA: W.B. Saunders Co. 1997
30. Orthopedic Foundation for Animals website: www.offa.com
31.a. Coates, Joan R., Kline, Karen L. Congenital and Inherited Neurologic Disorders in Dogs and Cats p. 11181118
31.b. Dunstan, Robert W., Hargis, Ann M. The Diagnosis of Sebaceous Adenitis in Standard Poodle Dogs. P 619 Kirk's Current Veterinary Therapy XII, Philadelphia, PA: W.B. Saunders Co. 1995
31. Genetics Committee of the American college of Veterinary Ophthalmologists, Ocular Disorders Presumed to be Inherited in Purebred Dogs. 5th ed. 2009
32. Ackerman, Lowell, The Genetic connection: a Guide to Health Problems in Purebred Dogs. Lakewood, CO, AAHA Press. 1999
33. Pomeranian Breed Requirements, Canine Health Information Center: www.caninehealthinfo.org
34. Buchanan, J.W. Prevalence of cardiovascular disorders. Textbook of Canine and Feline Cardiology, 2nd ed. Philadelphia, W.B. Saunders Co. 1999
35. Fleming, J.M., Creevy, K.E., Promislow, D.E.L. Mortality in North American Dogs from 1984 to 2004: an Investigation into Age-, Size-, and Breed-Related Causes of Death Journal of Veterinary Internal Medicine Vol. 25, Issue 2 March/April 2011 pages 187-198
36. LaFond, E., Breur, G.J., Austin, C.C. Breed susceptibility for developmental orthopedic diseases in dogs. J. Am Anim Hosp Assoc, 2002; 38:467-77
37. Hart, B.L., Hart, L. The Perfect Puppy, How to Choose Your Dog by Its Behavior New York, Barnes & Noble Books, 2001
38. Takeuchi, Y. Mori, Y. A Comparison of the Behavioral Profiles of Purebred Dogs in Japan to Profiles of those in the United States and the United Kingdom J Vet Med Sci 68 789-90 2006

NOTES

NOTES

www.ingramcontent.com/pod-product-compliance
Ingram Content Group UK Ltd.
Pitfield, Milton Keynes, MK11 3LW, UK
UKHW051313230126
10288UKWH00015B/47